Wild Animals
IN CROSS STITCH

·

Julie Burdon-Stone

MEREHURST

To John, my husband, whose love and encouragement gave me the confidence to follow my dreams.

THE CHARTS

Some of the designs in this book are very detailed and, due to inevitable space limitations, the charts may be shown on a comparatively small scale; in such cases, readers may find it helpful to have the particular chart with which they are currently working enlarged.

THREADS

The projects in this book were all stitched with Anchor stranded cotton embroidery threads. The keys given with each chart also list thread combinations for those who wish to use DMC or Madeira threads. It should be pointed out that the shades produced by different companies vary slightly, and it is not always possible to find identical colours in a different range.

Published in 1997 by Merehurst Limited
Ferry House, 51-57 Lacy Road, Putney, London SW15 1PR
Copyright © 1997 Merehurst Limited
ISBN 1 85391 536 X

A catalogue record for this book is available from the British Library.

Edited by Heather Dewhurst
Designed by Maggie Aldred
Photography by Juliet Piddington
Illustrations by John Hutchinson (pp5-7) and King & King (pp18 and 26)
Typesetting by Dacorum Type & Print, Hemel Hempstead
Colour separation by CH Colourscan, Malaysia
Printed in Hong Kong by Wing King Tong

Merehurst is the leading publisher of craft books and has an excellent range of titles to suit all levels. Please send to the address above for our free catalogue, stating the title of this book.

CONTENTS

INTRODUCTION

My love of wild animals has always inspired me to draw and paint. To have the opportunity to portray some of my favourites in cross stitch was a dream come true. I hope that you will enjoy stitching some of my animals, as much as I have enjoyed designing them. The projects featured in this book include ideas on how best to display your finished work, but most designs will work well simply framed as pictures.

Cross stitch is a popular and engaging hobby. The designs in this book use some of the many different-coloured Aidas in varying counts now available and explore some alternative evenweave fabrics.

I have endeavoured to include designs for all skill levels. For the beginner, there are the elephant and dolphin hand towel and luggage tag sets. The African safari cards and woodland trinket boxes will suit the intermediate stitchers and, for the more advanced, there is the absorbing tiger tray and the challenging polar bear picture.

For those of you who would like to use an alternative evenweave fabric, there are three designs for you to try: a chipmunk bookmark, a racoon address book cover and an otter spectacles case. However, any of the designs in this book can be reduced or enlarged, or the whole effect can be changed, simply by altering the count of the fabric, or using a different background colour.

We live in a busy stressful world, where mass-produced items are commonplace. What better way is there to unwind than to sit by a roaring fire in winter, or enjoy the warm summer sun, while stitching one of these animal designs for your home or as a gift for someone special.

BASIC SKILLS

BEFORE YOU BEGIN

PREPARING THE FABRIC
Even with an average amount of handling, many evenweave fabrics tend to fray at the edges, so it is a good idea to overcast the raw edges, using ordinary sewing thread, before you begin.

THE INSTRUCTIONS
Each project begins with a full list of the materials that you will require. Aida is a fabric produced by Zweigart. Note that the measurements given for the embroidery fabric include a minimum of 3cm (1¼in) all around to allow for stretching it in a frame and preparing the edges to prevent them from fraying.

Colour keys for stranded embroidery cottons – Anchor, DMC or Madeira – are given with each chart. It is assumed that you will need to buy one skein of each colour mentioned in a particular key, even though you may use less, but where two or more skeins are needed, this information is included in the main list of requirements.

To work from the charts, particularly those where several symbols are used in close proximity, some readers may find it helpful to have the chart enlarged so that the squares and symbols can be seen more easily. Many photocopying services will do this for a minimum charge.

Before you begin to embroider, always mark the centre of the design with two lines of basting stitches, one vertical and one horizontal, running from edge to edge of the fabric, as indicated by the arrows on the charts.

As you stitch, use the centre lines given on the chart and the basting threads on your fabric as reference points for counting the squares and threads to position your design accurately.

WORKING IN A HOOP
A hoop is the most popular frame for use with small areas of embroidery. It consists of two rings, one fitted inside the other; the outer ring usually has an

adjustable screw attachment so that it can be tightened to hold the stretched fabric in place. Hoops are available in several sizes, ranging from 10cm (4in) in diameter to quilting hoops with a diameter of 38cm (15in). Hoops with table stands or floor stands attached are also available.

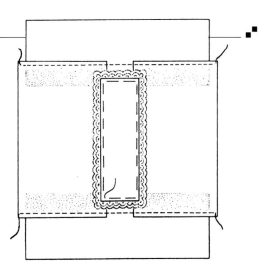

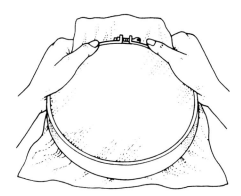

1 To stretch your fabric in a hoop, place the area to be embroidered over the inner ring and press the outer ring over it, with the tension screw released. Tissue paper can be placed between the outer ring and the embroidery, so that the hoop does not mark the fabric. Lay the tissue paper over the fabric when you set it in the hoop, then tear away the central embroidery area.

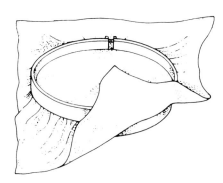

2 Smooth the fabric and, if necessary, straighten the grain before tightening the screw. The fabric should be evenly stretched.

EXTENDING EMBROIDERY FABRIC
It is easy to extend a piece of embroidery fabric, such as a bookmark, to stretch it in a hoop.

● Fabric oddments of a similar weight can be used. Simply cut four pieces to size (in other words, to the measurement that will fit both the embroidery fabric and your hoop) and baste them on each side of the embroidery fabric before stretching it in the hoop in the usual way.

WORKING IN A RECTANGULAR FRAME
Rectangular frames are more suitable for larger pieces of embroidery. They consist of two rollers, with tapes attached, and two flat side pieces, which slot into the rollers and are held in place by pegs or screw attachments. Available in different sizes, either alone or with adjustable table or floor stands, frames are measured by the length of the roller tape, and range in size from 30cm (12in) to 68cm (27in).

As alternatives to a slate frame, canvas stretchers and the backs of old picture frames can be used. Provided there is sufficient extra fabric around the finished size of the embroidery, the edges can be turned under and simply attached with drawing pins (thumb tacks) or staples.

1 To stretch your fabric in a rectangular frame, cut out the fabric, allowing at least an extra 5cm (2in) all around the finished size of the embroidery. Baste a single 12mm (½in) turning on the top and bottom edges and oversew strong tape, 2.5cm (1in) wide, to the other two sides. Mark the centre line both ways with basting stitches. Working from the centre outwards and using strong thread, oversew the top and bottom edges to the roller tapes. Fit the side pieces into the slots, and roll any extra fabric on one roller until the fabric is taut.

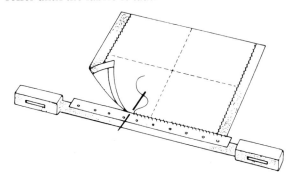

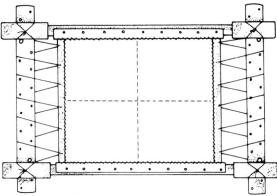

2 Insert the pegs or adjust the screw attachments to secure the frame. Thread a large-eyed needle (chenille needle) with strong thread or fine string and lace both edges, securing the ends around the intersections of the frame. Lace the webbing at 2.5cm (1in) intervals, stretching the fabric evenly.

BINDING AN EDGE

1 Open out the turning on one edge of the bias binding and pin in position on the right side of the fabric, matching the fold to the seamline. Fold over the cut end of the binding. Finish by overlapping the starting point by about 12mm (¹/₂in). Baste and machine stitch along the seamline.

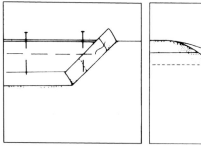

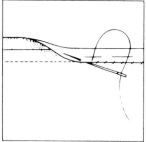

2 Fold the binding over the raw edge to the wrong side, baste and, using matching sewing thread, neatly hem to finish.

PIPED SEAMS

Contrasting piping adds a special decorative finish to a seam and looks particularly attractive on items such as cushions and cosies.

You can cover piping cord with either bias-cut fabric of your choice or a bias binding; alternatively, ready-covered piping cord is available in several widths and many colours.

1 To apply piping, pin and baste it to the right side of the fabric, with seam lines matching. Clip into the seam allowance where necessary.

2 With right sides together, place the second piece of fabric on top, enclosing the piping. Baste and then either hand stitch in place or machine stitch, using a zipper foot. Stitch as close to the piping as possible, covering the first line of stitching.

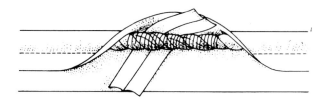

3 To join ends of piping cord together, first overlap the two ends by about 2.5cm (1in). Unpick the two cut ends of bias to reveal the cord. Join the bias strip as shown. Trim and press the seam open. Unravel and splice the two ends of the cord. Fold the bias strip over it, and finish basting around the edge.

MOUNTING EMBROIDERY

The cardboard should be cut to the size of the finished embroidery, with an extra 6mm (¹/₄in) added all around to allow for the recess in the frame.

LIGHTWEIGHT FABRICS

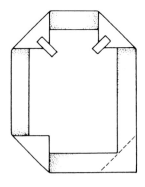

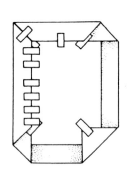

1 Place the embroidery face down, with the cardboard centred on top, and basting and pencil lines matching. Begin by folding over the fabric at each corner and securing it with masking tape.

2 Working first on one side and then the other, fold over the fabric on all sides and secure it firmly with pieces of masking tape, placed about 2.5cm (1in) apart. Also neaten the mitred corners with masking tape, pulling the fabric tightly to give a firm, smooth finish.

HEAVIER FABRICS

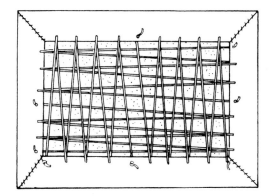

● Lay the embroidery face down, with the cardboard centred on top; fold over the edges of the fabric on opposite sides, making mitred folds at the corners, and lace across, using strong thread. Repeat on the other two sides. Finally, pull up the stitches fairly tightly to stretch the fabric firmly over the cardboard. Overstitch the mitred corners.

CROSS STITCH

For all cross stitch embroidery, the following two methods of working are used. In each case, neat rows of vertical stitches are produced on the back of the fabric.

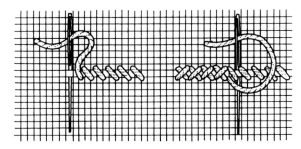

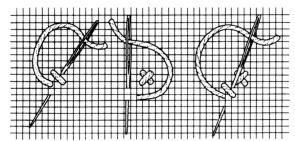

● When stitching large areas, work in horizontal rows. Working from right to left, complete the first row of evenly spaced diagonal stitches over the number of threads specified in the project instructions. Then, working from left to right, repeat the process. Continue in this way, making sure each stitch crosses in the same direction.

● When stitching diagonal lines, work downwards, completing each stitch before moving to the next.

BACKSTITCH

Backstitch is used in the projects to give emphasis to a particular foldline, an outline or a shadow. The stitches are worked over the same number of threads as the cross stitch, forming continuous straight or diagonal lines.

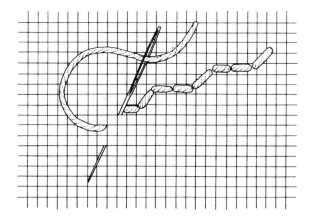

● Make the first stitch from left to right; pass the needle behind the fabric and bring it out one stitch length ahead to the left. Repeat and continue in this way along the line.

THREE-QUARTER CROSS STITCHES

Some fractional stitches are used on certain projects in this book; although they strike fear into the hearts of less experienced stitchers they are not difficult to master, and give a more natural line in certain instances. Should you find it difficult to pierce the centre of the Aida block, simply use a sharp needle to make a small hole in the centre first.

To work a three-quarter cross stitch, bring the needle up at point A and down through the centre of the square at B. Later, the diagonal backstitch finishes the stitch. Stitches worked in this way are indicated quite clearly on the charts with smaller-sized symbols.

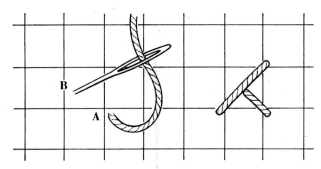

Tiger Drinks Tray

The tiger is the world's largest cat. Now close to extinction, this noble feline could soon exist only in zoos. Beautiful, courageous and oh-so-masculine, the tiger makes a perfect design for an evening drinks tray.

TIGER DRINKS TRAY

YOU WILL NEED

For the Tiger Drinks Tray design, mounted in a rosewood tray with an oval aperture measuring 30.5cm × 23cm (12¼in × 9¼in):

40cm × 30cm (16in × 12in) of ivory, 16-count Aida fabric
Stranded embroidery cotton in the colours given in the panel
No24 tapestry needle
Rosewood serving tray (for suppliers, see page 40)

●

THE EMBROIDERY

Prepare the fabric, marking the centre with basting stitches, following the instructions on page 4. As the design is relatively large, it is a good idea to use a frame to keep the work smooth; this will also make mounting easier when the embroidery is completed.

Find the centre of the chart and begin stitching, using two strands of cotton in the needle for the cross stitch, and stitching over one block of fabric. When you have completed all the cross stitch, work the backstitching. Backstitch is worked in both one and two strands in the colours listed (see the chart key).

If necessary, gently wash the completed work and press on the wrong side.

TIGER TRAY ▶		ANCHOR	DMC	MADEIRA
⌐	White	2	Blanc	White
⊟	Brown	351	400	2305
⊔	Copper brown	1049	3826	2306
X	Golden brown	307	783	2211
2	Yellow	300	745	0111
3	Grey	399	318	1802
4	Dark grey	400	317	1714
0	Black	403	310	Black
⊥	Dark golden brown	308	782	2212
▢	Salmon pink	9	352	0303
+	Rust brown	1002	977	2301
←	Forest green	267	470	1503
▽	Olive green	280	733	1611
●	Khaki	945	372	2110

Note: bks around tiger with one strand of black, around eyes and on top of nose with two strands of black. Work whiskers, eyebrows and chin whiskers in single large stitches with one strand of white.

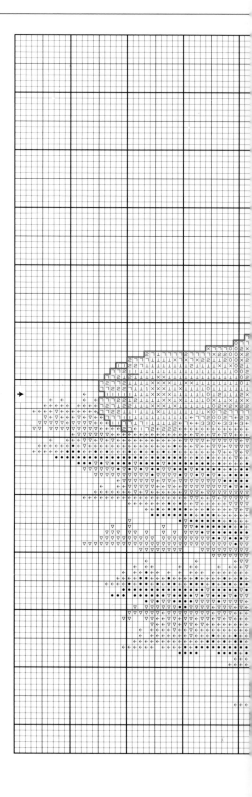

ASSEMBLING THE TRAY

Centre the design in the wooden oval mount and complete the assembly of the tray in accordance with the manufacturer's instructions.

Koala Cushion

Give your conservatory or sitting room a flavour of Australia with this cuddly koala cushion. Or, if you prefer, these shy and retiring marsupials would look just as good framed as a picture and hung in your favourite room.

KOALA CUSHION

For the Koala Cushion, measuring 35cm
(14in) square:

25cm (10in) square of ecru, 14-count Aida fabric
Stranded embroidery cotton in the colours given in
the panel
No24 tapestry needle
Two 41cm (16³/₈in) squares of plain pale green fabric,
for front and back of cushion
Matching pale green zip, 30cm (12in) long
Pale green sewing thread
Sewing needle
35cm (14in) square cushion pad
2m (2¹/₄yds) of pale brown piping cord

•

THE EMBROIDERY

Prepare the Aida fabric, marking the centre of the
material with basting stitches, then mount it in a
hoop or frame following the instructions on page 5.
Following the chart, start the embroidery at the
centre of the design, using two strands of embroidery
cotton in the needle for cross stitches and one strand
for backstitch. Work each stitch over a block of
fabric in each direction, making sure that all the top
crosses run in the same direction and each row is
worked into the same holes as the top or bottom of
the row before, so that you do not leave a space
between the rows.

MAKING UP THE COVER

When the design is completed, gently wash the
embroidered fabric and press on the wrong side.
Trim around the design, leaving 1.5cm (⁵/₈in) of
fabric and carefully baste the design onto the centre
of one of the squares of green material, turning
under the Aida border around the design as you go.
When the design is securely positioned, sew around
the edge in long and short stitches, using two strands
of dark brown embroidery cotton.

Cut the remaining square of green fabric in two
and baste the zip in position. Stitch it securely in
place; this is the back panel of the cushion.

Place the front panel of the cushion on the back
panel, with right sides facing; at this point make

sure that the zip is open. Baste, then sew around all
four sides, ensuring that the koala design remains
central. Trim the seams to about 1.5cm (⁵/₈in) when
completed. Turn the cover out to the right side and
press the back. Insert the cushion pad and close the
zip. Finally, slipstitch piping cord around the edge of
the cushion.

KOALA CUSHION ▶		ANCHOR	DMC	MADEIRA
⊓	Greyish-brown	393	3790	1905
—	Slate grey	235	414	1801
⊔	Charcoal grey	1041	844	1810
X	Green	216	3816	1311
0	Grey	399	318	1802
⊥	Black	403	310	Black
▢	White	2	Blanc	White
+	Pale grey	234	762	1804
↓	Dark grey	400	317	1714
←	Mid brown	374	420	2104
▽	Dark brown	906	829	2113
●	Light green	214	368	1310

*Note: bks around koala, including eyebrows, with charcoal grey, and
around the eyes and nose with black.*

14

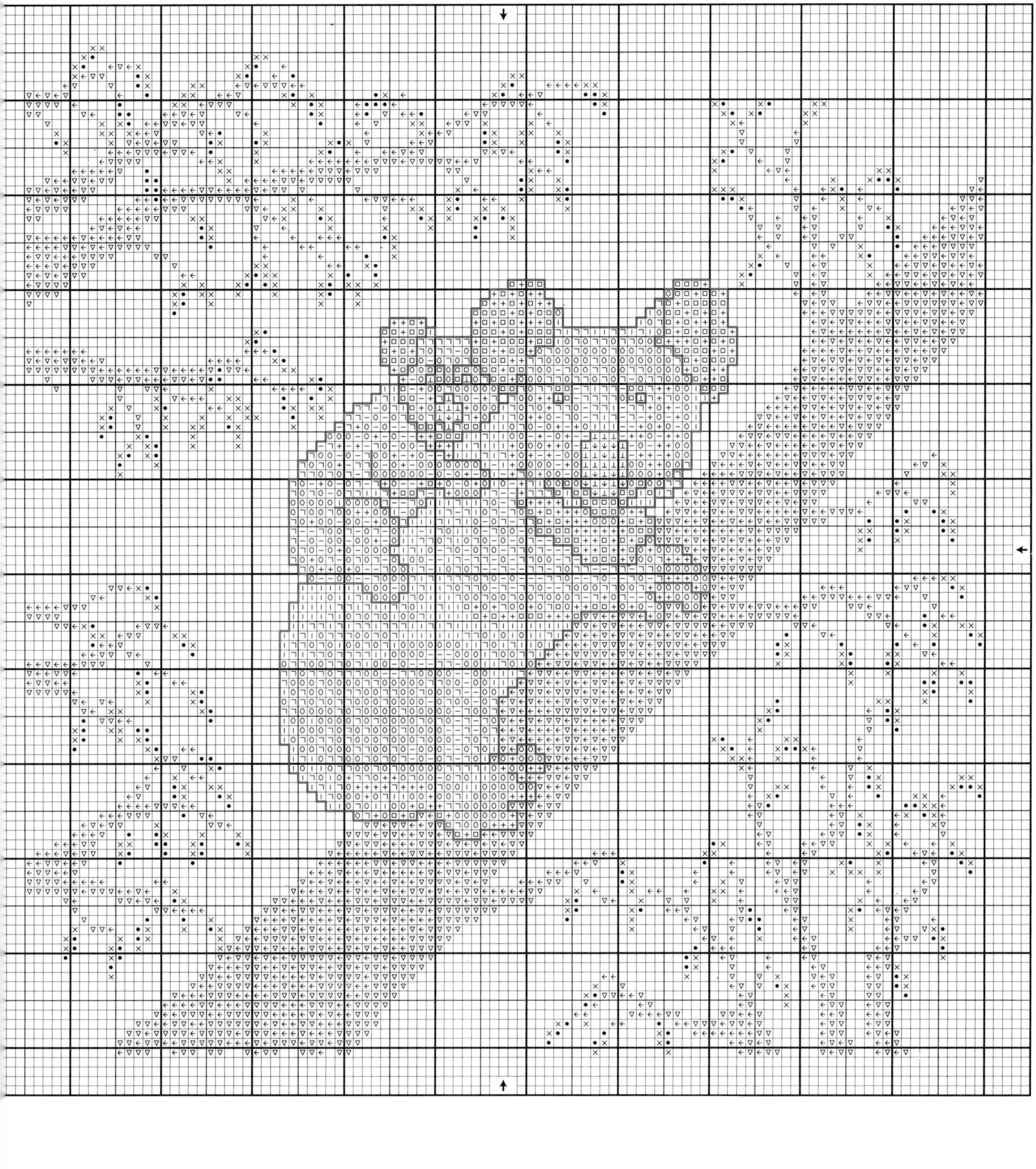

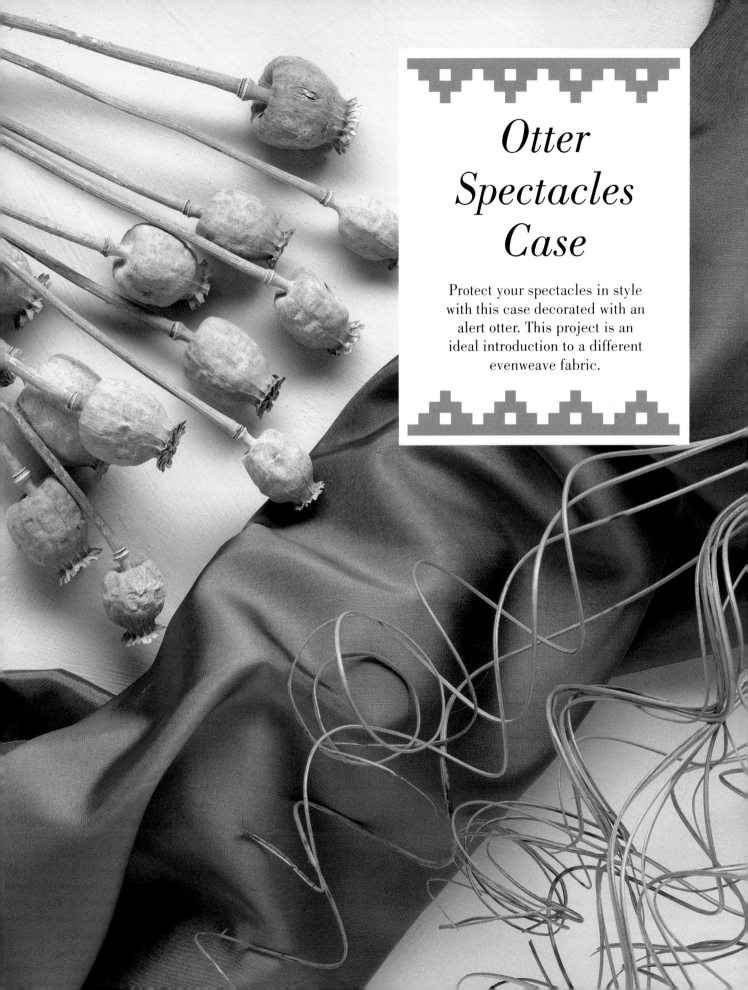

Otter Spectacles Case

Protect your spectacles in style with this case decorated with an alert otter. This project is an ideal introduction to a different evenweave fabric.

OTTER SPECTACLES CASE

YOU WILL NEED

For the Otter Spectacles Case, measuring
11cm × 18cm (4⅜in × 7¼in):

*Two pieces of 15cm × 23cm (6in × 9¼in) pale green,
28-count evenweave fabric
Stranded embroidery cotton in the colours given in
the panel
No24 tapestry needle
Medium-weight iron-on interfacing
Pale green sewing thread
Sewing needle
Two pieces of 13cm × 20cm (5¼in × 8in) dark green
felt, for lining the spectacles case
1m (40in) of thin midbrown piping cord*

•

THE EMBROIDERY

Take one piece of the evenweave fabric and mark the centre with basting stitches, following the instructions on page 4. Following the chart, start the embroidery at the centre of the design, using two strands of cotton for cross stitches and three-quarter stitches, and stitching over two threads of the fabric. There are several three-quarter stitches in the design (see page 7); these are easier to achieve on evenweave fabric, because the central hole is clearly visible. Three-quarter stitches are indicated on the chart by smaller symbols.

Once you have completed the cross stitches and three-quarter stitches, work the backstitching outline using one strand of cotton. Finally work the grass and reed stems as long stitches, using two strands of cotton.

MAKING THE SPECTACLES CASE

Press the completed otter design and iron the interfacing onto the back of the design. Take the second plain piece of evenweave fabric and iron the interfacing onto one side. Position the front and back panels of the case together, right sides facing, then baste and sew around the two long sides and the bottom, to the required size of the case, leaving 12mm (½in) along the top to turn over. The completed case should measure 11cm × 18cm (4⅜in × 7¼in). Trim off the excess fabric and press the seams. Turn the

case the right side out. Turn over the top to the inside and sew around the rim.

Pin the two pieces of felt together, then sew around the two long sides and the bottom. Trim off the excess fabric. Carefully slot the felt lining into the otter case; when it is in position, carefully sew into place on top of the hem. Finally slipstitch cord piping around the three sides of the case and around the front and back rim.

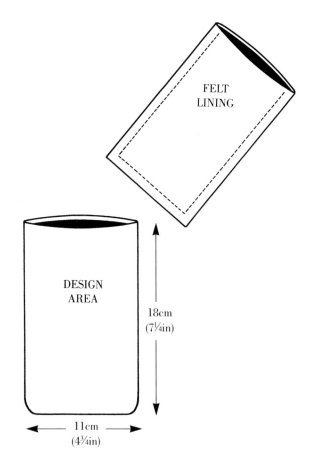

FELT LINING

DESIGN AREA

18cm (7¼in)

11cm (4¾in)

OTTER SPECTACLES CASE ▶	ANCHOR	DMC	MADEIRA
△ Ecru	387	Ecru	Ecru
Z Pale grey	398	415	1803
Ⅱ Peach	347	402	2312
⟍ Yellowish-green	874	834	2204
3 Chestnut brown	349	301	2306
■ Black	403	310	Black
9 Cream	926	712	2101
▢ Greyish-brown	898	611	2107
X Dark greyish-brown	889	610	2106
▲ Charcoal brown	905	3021	1904
⟍ Moss green	245	700	1214
S Green	242	989	1401

Note: bks around otter with black. Work the bulrush stems in long stitch using moss green, and the long grass in long stitch using yellowish-green and green.

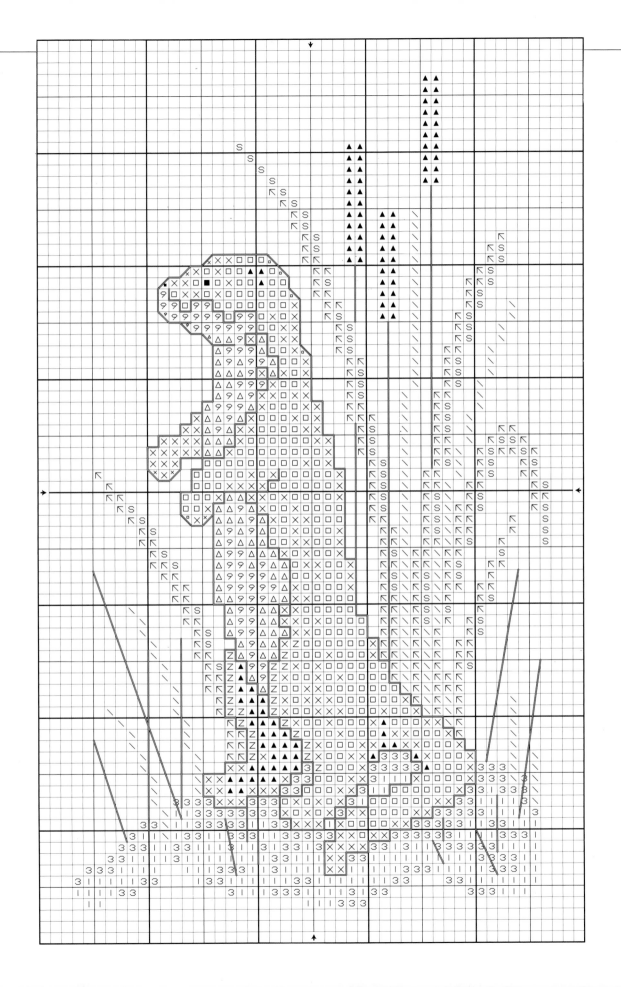

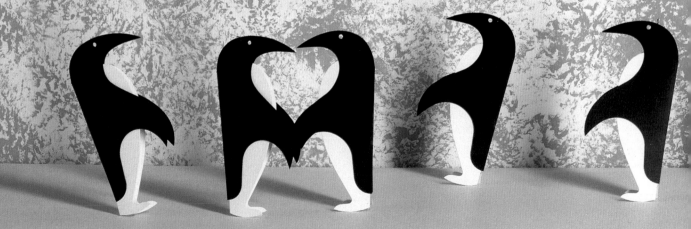

Polar Bear Picture

Under a clear and starry sky
in the Arctic, a female polar bear
and her cubs pad softly across
a frozen glacier. What better way to
while away the long winter evenings
than to sew this striking picture.

POLAR BEAR PICTURE

YOU WILL NEED

For the Polar Bear Picture, mounted in a wooden rectangular frame with an aperture measuring 38cm × 20cm (15¼in × 8in):

50cm × 30cm (20in × 12in) of navy, 14-count Aida fabric
Stranded embroidery cotton in the colours given in the panel
No24 tapestry needle
Stiff cardboard, for mounting
Frame and mount of your choice

•

THE EMBROIDERY

Prepare the fabric, marking the centre with basting stitches, following the instructions on page 4. This design is quite large, so it is recommended that you use a frame to keep the work taut; this also makes it easier to mount and frame the embroidery once it is completed.

Following the chart, start the embroidery at the centre of the design, using three strands of cotton for stitching the polar bears, and two strands for the rest of the cross stitches and three-quarter stitches, and stitching over one block of the fabric. Using three strands of thread for the polar bears gives them a more solid colour, making their fur appear thick and soft.

When you have completed the cross stitching, work the backstitch highlighting on the polar bears' noses using one strand of thread. When completed, gently wash the picture and press on the wrong side.

ASSEMBLING THE PICTURE

Centre the design over the cardboard mount and fix in place, following the instructions on page 6. Place the mount, picture and backing board into the frame, then secure and seal with masking tape.

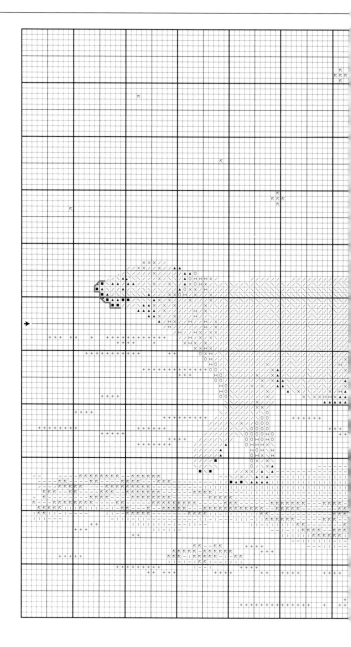

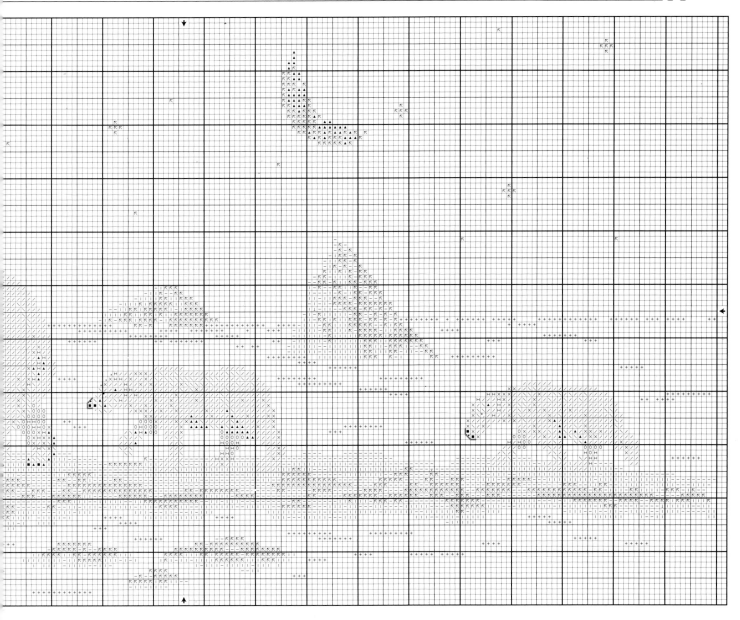

POLAR BEAR ▲ PICTURE	ANCHOR	DMC	MADEIRA
H Fawn	891	676	2208
− Turquoise	168	807	1109
I Deep blue	169	3809	1108
⊼ Pale blue	1037	3756	2504
⁄ White	2	Blanc	White
■ Black	403	310	Black
0 Dark fawn	890	729	2209
X Yellow	301	744	0112
＼ Pale grey	234	762	1804
▲ Grey	399	318	1802
+ Blue	136	799	0910

Note: bks around polar bears' noses with white.

Book Cover and Bookmark

Both of these simple projects conjure up images of North American forests, where the chipmunk and racoon are still commonly found.

BOOK COVER AND BOOKMARK

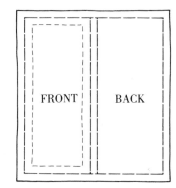

YOU WILL NEED

For the Racoon Address Book Cover, measuring
9cm × 17cm (3½in × 6¾in):

*30cm × 25cm (12in × 10in) of light blue, 28-count
evenweave fabric
Stranded embroidery cotton in the colours given in
the appropriate panel
No24 tapestry needle
Medium-weight iron-on interfacing
Address book, approximately 9cm × 17cm
(3½in × 6¾in)
Double-sided sticky tape
Coloured sticky tape or masking tape*

For the Chipmunk Bookmark, measuring
6cm × 19cm (2⅜in × 7½in):

*15cm × 25cm (6in × 10in) of light blue, 28-count
evenweave fabric·
Stranded embroidery cotton in the colours given in
the appropriate panel
No24 tapestry needle
Medium-weight iron-on interfacing
6cm × 19cm (2⅜in × 7½in) of plain white, stiff
cardboard
Double-sided sticky tape
65cm (26in) of light blue ribbon*

•

THE EMBROIDERY

Baste the edges of the fabric for the address book
cover, and mark the edges of the design area on the
right side of the fabric with basting stitches, allowing
a minimum border of 2.5cm (1in) around the top,
bottom and right side of the design (see the diagram). Mount the fabric in a hoop or small frame and
stitch the design in the colours listed, following the
chart. Work all the cross stitches first using two
strands of cotton, then complete the backstitch using
one strand of cotton. Finally, work the long stitches
using two strands of cotton. When completed, wash
the embroidered fabric if necessary and press it on
the wrong side, then iron the interfacing on the back
of the design.

To make the bookmark, baste the edges of the
material and mark the centre with a stitch, then
mount it in a hoop or small frame and complete the
stitching, following the chart. Work the cross stitches
first, using two strands of cotton, then work the
backstitching, using one strand of cotton. When finished, press the work on the wrong side and iron the
interfacing on the back.

MAKING UP THE ADDRESS BOOK COVER

Place the embroidery face down, and lay the front of
the address book on top; carefully position the
design by drawing gently around the book on the
interfacing. Attach the embroidery to the address
book using strips of double-sided sticky tape. When
the outside of the book is covered, trim the excess
fabric, leaving a 2.5cm (1in) border. Then fold over
the corners and stick them down firmly with double-
sided tape, and complete by folding over the remaining fabric. Finally, cover the raw edges of the fabric
on the inside of the cover with coloured sticky tape
or masking tape, to prevent it from fraying.

MAKING UP THE BOOKMARK

Place the embroidery face down and stick the piece
of cardboard over the back of the design, using
double-sided sticky tape. Fold the excess fabric
around the card and stick it down on the back (see
the diagram) using double-sided sticky tape. Secure
the end flaps with slipstitches if necessary, then
attach the ribbon with sticky tape over the centre
join on the back.

RACOON ADDRESS BOOK COVER ▼

		ANCHOR	DMC	MADEIRA
●	Ecru	387	Ecru	Ecru
R	Pale grey	398	415	1803
▲	Slate grey	235	414	1801
F	Olive green	279	734	1610
5	Lime green	255	907	1410
■	Black	403	310	Black
2	White	2	Blanc	White
0	Charcoal	1041	844	1810
–	Beige	372	738	2013
/	Very pale grey	234	762	1804
T	Green	257	905	1412
J	Chestnut brown	349	301	2306
↖	Rust brown	1001	976	2302
X	Dark brown	358	801	2007

Note: bks around racoon with one strand of black, and bird with two strands of black. Work the long grass as long stitches with rust brown, green and olive green.

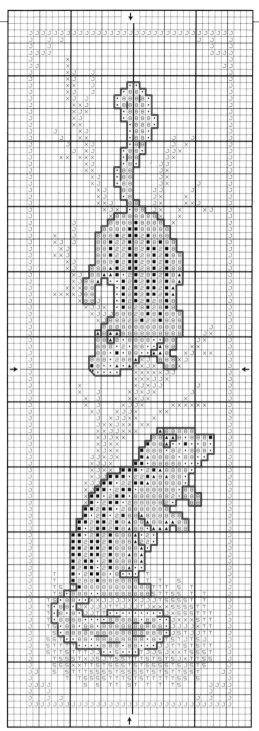

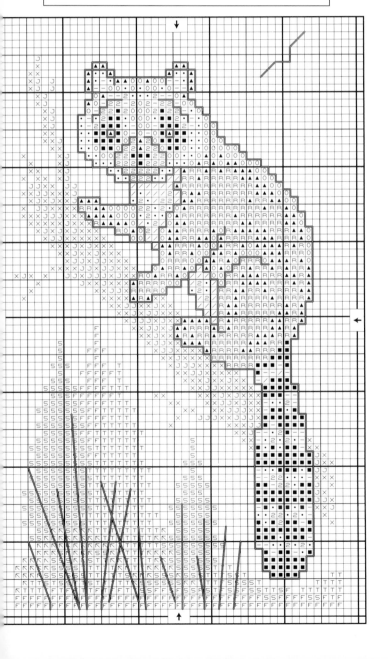

CHIPMUNK ▲ BOOKMARK

		ANCHOR	DMC	MADEIRA
2	White	2	Blanc	White
X	Dark brown	358	801	2007
T	Green	257	905	1412
■	Black	403	310	Black
8	Greyish brown	393	3790	1905
●	Ecru	387	Ecru	Ecru
▲	Slate grey	235	414	1801
J	Chestnut brown	349	301	2306
5	Lime green	255	907	1410

Note: bks around chipmunks with black.

Safari Greetings Cards

Send a taste of Africa to family and friends with these safari greetings cards. Suitable for most occasions, these small projects are an ideal introduction to 18-count Aida.

SAFARI GREETINGS CARDS

YOU WILL NEED

For the Zebra Card, measuring 15cm × 20cm (6in × 8in), with a circular aperture measuring 10cm (4in) in diameter:

15cm (6in) square of light blue, 18-count Aida fabric
Stranded embroidery cotton in the colours listed in the appropriate panel
No24 tapestry needle
Medium-weight iron-on interfacing
Cream greetings card blank (for suppliers, see page 40)
Double-sided sticky tape

For the Hippo Card, measuring 15cm × 20cm (6in × 8in), with a square aperture measuring 10cm (4in):

15cm (6in) square of light blue, 18-count Aida fabric
Stranded embroidery cotton in the colours listed in the appropriate panel
No24 tapestry needle
Medium-weight iron-on interfacing
Cream greetings card blank (for suppliers, see page 40)
Double-sided sticky tape

For the Lion Card, measuring 15cm × 10cm (6in × 4in), with a rectangular aperture measuring 11cm × 7cm (4¾in × 2¾in):

15cm × 11cm (6in × 4¾in) of cream, 18-count Aida fabric
Stranded embroidery cotton in the colours listed in the appropriate panel
No24 tapestry needle
Medium-weight iron-on interfacing
Pale blue greetings card blank (for suppliers, see page 40)
Double-sided sticky tape

For the Giraffe Card, measuring 10cm × 15cm (4in × 6in), with an oval aperture measuring 7.5cm × 11.5cm (3in × 4½in):

11cm × 15cm (4¾in × 6in) of cream, 18-count Aida fabric
Stranded embroidery cotton in the colours listed in the appropriate panel
No24 tapestry needle
Medium-weight iron-on interfacing
Pale blue greetings card blank (for suppliers, see page 40)
Double-sided sticky tape

●

THE EMBROIDERY

The following instructions apply to all of the cards. First baste the edges of the material and mark the centre with a loose basting stitch, following the instructions on page 4. Secure the material in a hoop or small frame, then find the centre of the chart and begin stitching, using two strands of cotton in the needle for the cross stitch, and stitching over one block of fabric. When you have completed the cross stitching, work the backstitching. Outlining is

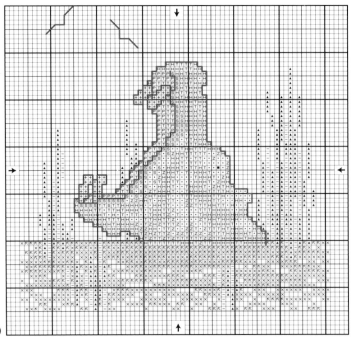

HIPPO CARD ◀		ANCHOR	DMC	MADEIRA
●	Dark pink	894	3688	0813
S	Pale pink	892	3774	0501
X	Indigo	169	3809	1108
◣	Dark indigo	170	3808	2505
■	Black	403	310	Black
H	Dark grey	236	3799	1713
T	Slate grey	235	414	1801
+	Pale lemon	386	3823	0101
Z	Dark fawn	890	729	2209
P	Pink	36	3326	0504
▲	Green	244	987	1403
−	Ochre	907	832	2202

Note: bks around hippo with one strand of dark grey, and birds with one strand of black.

worked mostly in one strand of cotton although two strands have been used in various parts of the designs; refer to the individual keys for more detail.

MAKING UP THE CARDS

Press the completed design, then cut a piece of interfacing to the appropriate size and iron it on to the back of the work. Carefully trim around the edges, until the design fits comfortably into the card, with the design centred in the aperture. Secure with double-sided sticky tape. Cover and seal the back of the design with the card flap, securing with several small pieces of double-sided sticky tape.

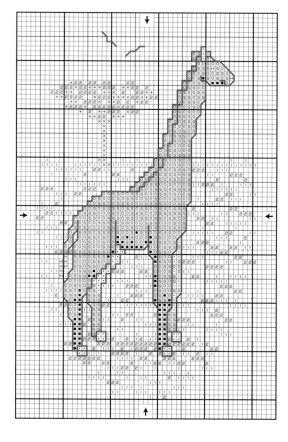

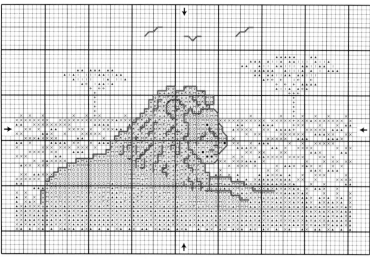

ZEBRA CARD ▲		ANCHOR	DMC	MADEIRA
●	Yellowish-green	874	834	2204
❘	Slate grey	235	414	1801
+	Forest green	267	470	1503
4	Grey	399	318	1802
■	Black	403	310	Black
2	White	2	Blanc	White
X	Olive green	280	733	1611
▼	Dark forest green	268	937	1504
Z	Light greyish-brown	832	612	2108
╱	Fawn	366	739	2014

Note: bks around zebra and birds with one strand of black. Outline zebra's eye with two strands of black.

GIRAFFE CARD ◀		ANCHOR	DMC	MADEIRA
■	Ecru	276	Ecru	Ecru
2	Forest green	267	470	1503
X	Greyish-brown	832	612	2108
H	Black	403	310	Black
0	Brown	365	780	2010
S	Beige	361	738	2013
●	Grey	399	318	1802
❘	Olive green	279	734	1610
+	Dark forest green	268	937	1504

Note: bks around giraffe and birds with one strand of black.

LION CARD ▶		ANCHOR	DMC	MADEIRA
M	Sand	306	3820	2514
▲	Forest green	267	470	1503
X	Olive green	279	734	1610
❘	Dark forest green	268	937	1504
■	Black	403	310	Black
0	Yellow	305	725	0108
⬉	Brown	310	434	2009
+	Cream	275	746	0101
↓	Dark golden brown	308	782	2212
⬅	Greyish-brown	832	612	2108

Note: bks around lion and birds with one strand of black.

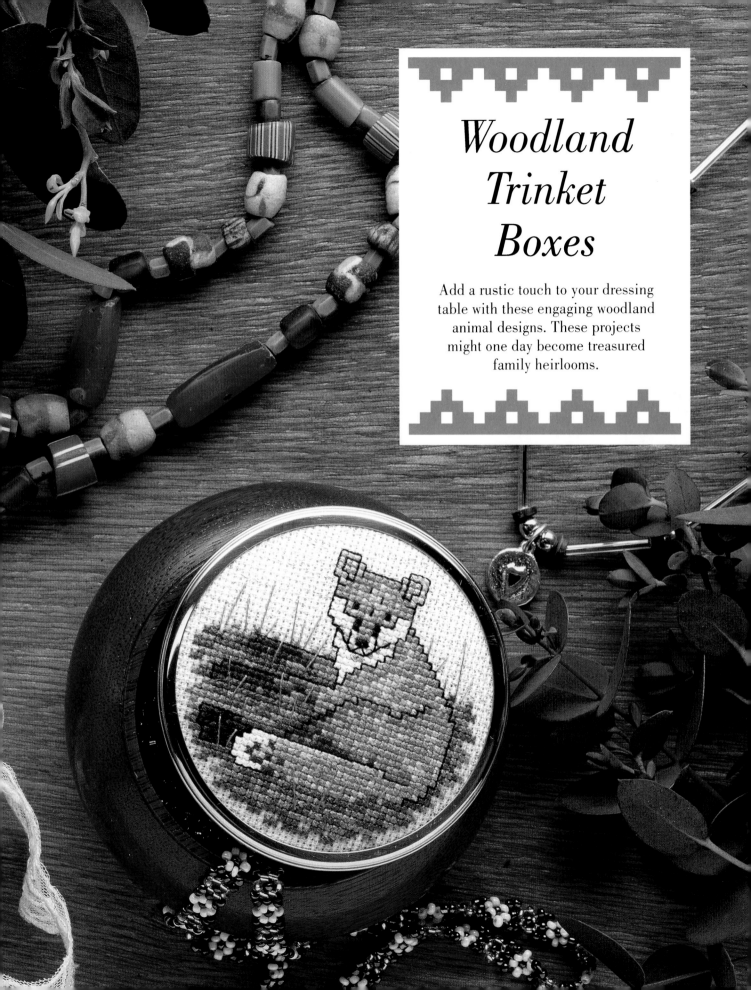

Woodland Trinket Boxes

Add a rustic touch to your dressing table with these engaging woodland animal designs. These projects might one day become treasured family heirlooms.

WOODLAND TRINKET BOXES

YOU WILL NEED

For the Squirrel Trinket Box, with a 3cm (1¼in)
diameter top:

8cm (3¼in) square of rustico, 18-count Aida fabric
Stranded embroidery cotton in the colours listed in
the appropriate panel
No24 tapestry needle
Medium-weight iron-on interfacing
Small rosewood bowl (for suppliers, see page 40)

For the Fox Trinket Box, with a 7cm (2¾in)
diameter top:

12cm (4¾in) square of rustico, 18-count Aida fabric
Stranded embroidery cotton in the colours listed in
the appropriate panel
No24 tapestry needle
Medium-weight iron-on interfacing
Medium rosewood bowl (for suppliers, see page 40)

For the Fawn Trinket Box, with a 9cm (3½in)
diameter top:

15cm (6in) square of rustico, 18-count Aida fabric
Stranded embroidery cotton in the colours listed in
the appropriate panel
No24 tapestry needle
Medium-weight iron-on interfacing
Large rosewood bowl (for suppliers, see page 40)

•

THE EMBROIDERY

Baste the edges of the material and secure in a hoop
or small frame, following the instructions on page 5.
Work all the cross stitches first, using two strands of
cotton, then complete the backstitch, using one
strand of cotton. Finally, work the grass strands in
single long stitches using two strands of cotton.

MAKING UP THE TRINKET BOXES

Press the completed designs, then iron the interfacing onto the back of each design. Place each design
face down and draw around the lid of the trinket box
on the back of the interfacing. Carefully cut away the
excess material, making sure that the design is
centred in the metal frame. Then complete the
assembly, according to the manufacturer's instructions.

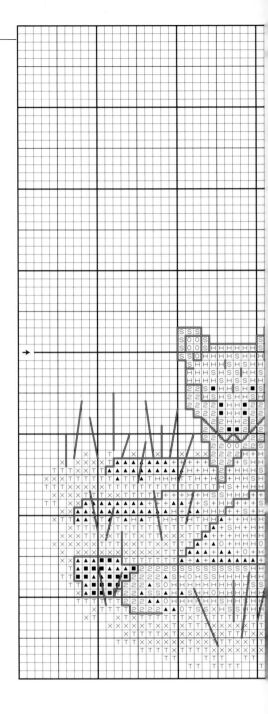

FOX TRINKET BOX ▲		ANCHOR	DMC	MADEIRA
▲	Dark brown	381	938	2005
0	Grey	399	318	1802
■	Black	403	310	Black
H	Tan	365	780	2010
2	White	2	Blanc	White
+	Dark tan	355	975	2303
S	Sandy brown	363	3827	2301
X	Green	243	988	1402
T	Moss green	245	700	1214

*Note: bks around fox with black, and work long grass as single long
stitches with green.*

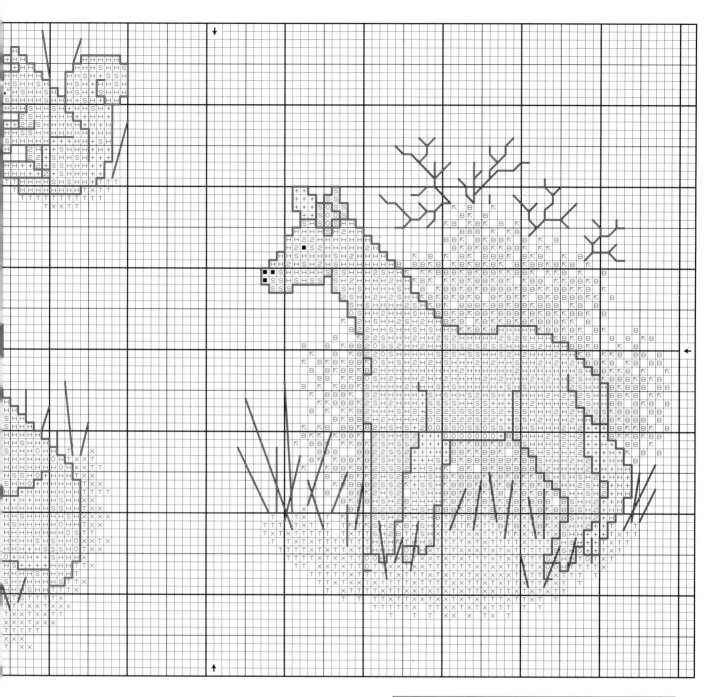

SQUIRREL ▲ TRINKET BOX

		ANCHOR	DMC	MADEIRA
■	Black	403	310	Black
H	Tan	365	780	2010
2	White	2	Blanc	White
+	Dark tan	355	975	2303
S	Sandy brown	363	3827	2301
X	Green	243	988	1402
T	Moss green	245	700	1214

Note: bks around squirrel with black, and work long grass as single long stitches with green.

FAWN TRINKET ▲ BOX

		ANCHOR	DMC	MADEIRA
▲	Dark brown*	381	938	2005
0	Grey	399	318	1802
B	Light green	266	471	1501
↖	Olive green	279	734	1610
■	Black	403	310	Black
H	Tan	365	780	2010
2	White	2	Blanc	White
+	Dark tan	355	975	2303
S	Sandy brown	363	3827	2301
X	Green	243	988	1402
T	Moss green	245	700	1214

Note: bks around fawn with black, and twigs of tree with dark brown (* used for bks only). Work long grass as single long stitches with green.*

Elephant and Dolphin Motifs

Elephants and dolphins are firm favourites with animal lovers the world over. These simple projects will make a very useful addition to your holiday luggage.

ELEPHANT AND DOLPHIN MOTIFS

YOU WILL NEED

For the Elephant Hand Towel, measuring
26cm × 46cm (10⅜in × 18⅜in):

*One cream hand towel with a 25cm × 6cm
(10in × 2⅜in) 14-count Aida band (for suppliers,
see page 40)
Stranded embroidery cotton in the colours listed in
the appropriate panel
No24 tapestry needle*

For the Dolphin Hand Towel, measuring
26cm × 46cm (10⅜in × 18⅜in):

*One light blue hand towel with a 25cm × 6cm
(10in × 2⅜in) 14-count Aida band (for suppliers,
see page 40)
Stranded embroidery cotton in the colours listed in
the appropriate panel
No24 tapestry needle*

For the Elephant Luggage Tag, measuring
8cm × 5cm (3¼in × 2in), and with a design aperture
measuring 7cm × 4.5cm (2¾in × 1¼in):

*12cm × 10cm (4¾in × 4in) of cream,
18-count Aida fabric
Stranded embroidery cotton in the colours listed in
the appropriate panel
No24 tapestry needle
Lightweight iron-on interfacing
Clear plastic luggage tag (for suppliers, see page 40)*

For the Dolphin Luggage Tag, measuring
8cm × 5cm (3¼in × 2in), and with a design aperture
measuring 7cm × 4.5cm (2¾in × 1¼in):

*12cm × 10cm (4¾in × 4in) of light blue,
18-count Aida fabric
Stranded embroidery cotton in the colours listed in
the appropriate panel
No24 tapestry needle
Lightweight iron-on interfacing
Clear plastic luggage tag (for suppliers, see page 40)*

●

THE EMBROIDERY

To sew the hand towels, it is recommended that you
use a frame to avoid creasing (see page 5). Carefully
attach the towel to a frame and find the centre on the
Aida band. Following the chart, begin stitching,
using two strands of cotton for the cross stitch and
stitching over one block of fabric. When you have
completed the cross stitches, work the backstitches
using one strand of cotton. Gently press the finished
work on the wrong side.

To sew the luggage tags, first baste the edges of
the fabric, then find the centre and stitch as above,
completing the backstitch last. Press the embroidered fabric when completed.

ASSEMBLING THE LUGGAGE TAGS

Iron the interfacing onto the back of each design,
then place the removable plastic panel of the
luggage tag over the design and mark around it in
pencil. Trim off any excess fabric and place the
embroidery in the luggage tag, with any backing
paper or card for an address behind the design.
Secure with the remaining plastic panel.

ELEPHANT HAND TOWEL ▶ & LUGGAGE TAG		ANCHOR	DMC	MADEIRA
■	Black	403	310	Black
2	White	2	Blanc	White
X	Forest green	267	470	1503
H	Charcoal	1041	844	1810
0	Grey	900	648	1814
S	Greyish-brown	393	3790	1905
I	Dark grey	8581	646	1812
+	Olive green	280	733	1611

Note: bks around elephants with charcoal, and birds with black.

DOLPHIN HAND TOWEL ▶ & LUGGAGE TAG		ANCHOR	DMC	MADEIRA
■	Black	403	310	Black
2	White	2	Blanc	White
X	Blue	162	825	1011
□	Pale grey	234	762	1804
9	Grey	399	318	1802
▲	Slate grey	235	414	1801
S	Dark grey	400	317	1714

Note: bks around dolphins and birds with black.

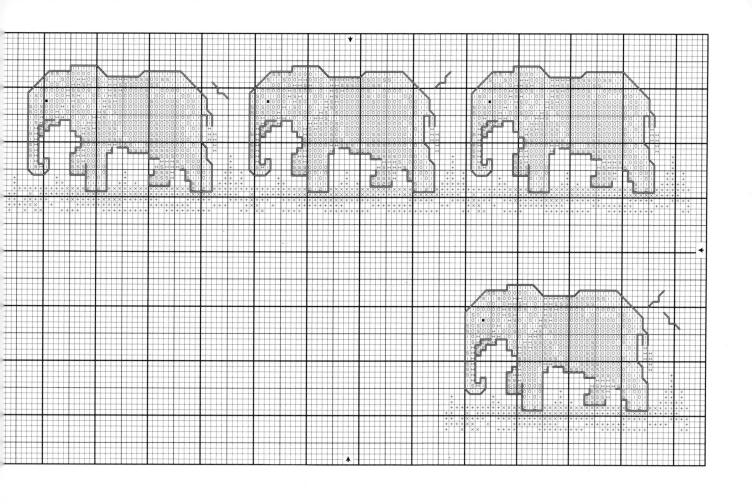

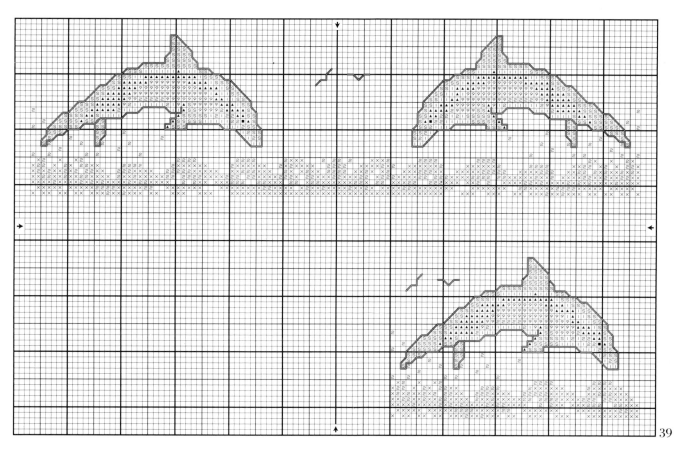

ACKNOWLEDGEMENTS

I would like to say a special thank you to the following people:

My husband John for his help and patience; my mother Doreen Burdon who inspired me to sew; Lynn Bates and all at *Needlework* magazine for starting me off; Ian and Martin of IL-Soft for their brilliant computer program; Framecraft Miniatures Limited for supplying their products used in this book; and, finally, to Karen Hemingway at Merehurst for giving me such a wonderful project.

SUPPLIERS

The following companies have supplied some of the items needed to complete various projects in this book.

For the Rosewood Tray, Woodland Trinket Boxes and Luggage Tags:
Framecraft Miniatures Limited
372-376 Summer Lane
Hockley
Birmingham B19 3QA
Telephone: 0121 212 0551

For all the Aida and Hand Towels:
Willow Fabrics
27 Willow Green
Knutsford
Cheshire WA16 6AX
Telephone: 01565 621 098

Craft Creations Limited
Units 1-7 Harpers Yard
Ruskin Road
Tottenham
London N17 8QA
Telephone: 0181 885 2655

Addresses for Framecraft stockists worldwide
Ireland Needlecraft Pty Ltd
2-4 Keppel Drive
Hallam, Victoria 3803
Australia

Danish Art Needlework
PO Box 442, Lethbridge
Alberta T1J 3Z1
Canada

Sanyei Imports
PO Box 5, Hashima Shi
Gifu 501-62
Japan

The Embroidery Shop
286 Queen Street
Masterton
New Zealand

Anne Brinkley Designs Inc.
246 Walnut Street
Newton
Mass. 02160
USA

S A Threads and Cottons Ltd
43 Somerset Road
Cape Town
South Africa

For information on your nearest stockist of embroidery cotton, contact the following:

DMC
(also distributors of Zweigart fabrics)

UK
DMC Creative World Limited
62 Pullman Road, Wigston
Leicester LE8 2DY
Telephone: 0116 2811040

USA
The DMC Corporation
Port Kearney Bld.
10 South Kearney
NJ 07032-0650
Telephone: 201 589 0606

AUSTRALIA
DMC Needlecraft Pty
PO Box 317
Earlswood 2206
NSW 2204
Telephone: 02599 3088

COATS AND ANCHOR
UK
Coats Paton Crafts
McMullen Road
Darlington
Co. Durham DL1 1YQ
Telephone: 01325 381010

USA
Coats & Clark
PO Box 27067
Dept CO1
Greenville SC 29616
Telephone: 803 234 0103

AUSTRALIA
Coats Patons Crafts
Thistle Street
Launceston
Tasmania 7250
Telephone: 00344 4222

MADEIRA

UK
Madeira Threads (UK) Limited
Thirsk Industrial Park
York Road, Thirsk
N. Yorkshire YO7 3BX
Telephone: 01845 524880

USA
Madeira Marketing Limited
600 East 9th Street
Michigan City
IN 46360
Telephone: 219 873 1000

AUSTRALIA
Penguin Threads Pty Limited
25-27 Izett Street
Prahran
Victoria 3181
Telephone: 03529 4400